CONTENTS

"I write about love a lot. Our feelings about love
over hundreds of years have not changed,
so I must say the same thing differently,
in a way that everyone can understand."

Paul Williams

Introduction

"There's a great comfort in writing something," says Paul Williams. "You're giving vent to your feelings and, if somebody else relates to them, there is a great comfort in that."

People have been listening and relating to Paul Williams' lyrics for over ten years and finding a wealth of comfort, appreciation and understanding in his words and melodies. Paul has successfully translated the passion of life into poetic expressions which are known and loved by fans of all ages and backgrounds. His songs — compositions like "We've Only Just Begun," "Rainy Days and Mondays" and "Out in the Country" — are familiar throughout the world, thanks to their universal appeal — expressing the wonder and joy of love and life.

You and Me Against the World showcases the pure beauty of Paul's songs and presents them as a testament of an important contemporary poetic voice. Susan Polis Schutz's selection of lyrics and Stephen Schutz's heart-warming illustrations complete this special collection.

In the pages to follow, you'll find an assortment of old stand-bys and new-found favorites waiting to be discovered. *You and Me Against the World* welcomes you into the expressive world of Paul Williams.

Every act of kindness
is a little bit of love
we leave behind
every summer sun
that has passed our way
serves to light every day . . .
so when we have gone
what we do lives on
you know
every act of kindness
is a little bit of love
we leave behind

If we change, we'll change together
Pick up the pieces if our dreams
  should fall
Put them back again together
We've found the love to mend
  them all

We've only just begun to live

e've only just begun to live
White lace and promises
A kiss for luck
 and we're on our way

Before the rising sun we fly
So many roads to choose
We start out walking and learn to run
And yes, we've just begun

Sharing horizons that are new to us
Watching the signs along the way
Talking it over just the two of us
Working together day to day
Together

And when the evening comes we smile
So much of life ahead
We'll find a place where there's room to grow
And yes, we've just begun

You're a night of rest
   when I am stumbling and tired
You're the patience
   that I never learned
You're a fresh idea
   when I'm feeling uninspired
You're the honors
   that I never earned . . .

You urge me on
You know me better,
   even better than I know myself . . .
Stand by me

I won't last a day without you

**W**hen you're near my love
If all my friends have forgotten
Half their promises
They're not unkind
Just hard to find
One look at you
And I know that I could learn to live
Without the rest
I found the best

When there's no getting over that rainbow
When my smallest of dreams won't come true
I can take all the madness the world has to give
But I won't last a day without you

**F**ollow your heart
Like the path of an arrow
That looks for a home
In the morning sky
Out of the nest
Like a small summer sparrow
That knows in his heart
He was born to fly

've kept you in my heart
    every hour
    that we're apart . . .
The times I've known
    counting the stars alone
Alone I've come to be somebody waiting

Promise me as you travel each mile
You'll think of me every once in awhile
I feel the sunshine
    in the warmth of your smile

Some sleepless night
If you should find yourself alone
Let me be the one you run to . . .
To set things right
When this old world's turned upside down
Let me be the one you run to . . .
For love and understanding
To find a quiet place
For silent understanding
A loving touch
Come to me when things go wrong
And there's no love to light the way

Let me be the one you run to
Let me be the one you come to
When you need someone to turn to
Let me be the one

Rainy days and Mondays always get me down . . .

Talkin' to myself and feelin' old
Sometimes I'd like to quit
Nothing ever seems to fit
Hangin' around
Nothing to do but frown
Rainy days and Mondays always get me down

What I've got they used to call the blues
Nothing is really wrong
Feelin' like I don't belong
Walkin' around
Some kind of lonely clown
Rainy days and Mondays always get me down

Funny but it seems
I always wind up here with you
Nice to know somebody loves me
Funny but it seems
That it's the only thing to do
Run and find the one who loves me

What I feel has come and gone before
No need to talk it out
We know what it's all about
Hangin' around
Nothing to do but frown
Rainy days and Mondays always get me down

ome days it don't pay
To get up out of bed
Seems like
    the whole world's
    Overworked and underfed
But life is loaded with sweet surprises
You never know what it will do
And just when you're plannin' on
Another rainy day
The sun comes shinin' through

n a world of hidden treasure
I have found the rainbow,
found it in you.
Taking comfort
    in your pleasure
love will come in silence, faithful and true.

Like a child
Who's learned the ways of life
You opened up my eyes
With a love that's always new
Yes I owe it all to you
'Cause when the world outside
Was sure that I was only chasing rainbows
You could find the words
To make me strong

Holding on to me and whispering
"There's nothing wrong with rainbows"
You heard my song
And so remember me
As one who came to love
And found a perfect love . . .
       along the way

Brighter than sunshine reflected on water
The smile of the lady is gracious and warm . . .
Sharing my secrets and wishing my wishes
A whisper of summer is there in her smile
Softly reflecting our love in the things that we say

s it wrong to say
I love you right away
to somebody new
even though you know you do
You decide what's right for you
and I'll decide for me
You know where you're comin' from
and where you'd like to be
All of us are different
as the snowflakes from the sky
Snow was born to fall
We were born to fly

Let's ride aboard a windy day
We can hide behind the clouds
And disappear
Sunshine can be so near
It's a crime to throw your time away
When the world is ours
And there's so much to see . . .

Are you with me
We can run for the sun
We'll try to find a place that is right
For us to laugh our time away
Try to find a place out of sight
For us to settle down and stay

As I have come to you
receive and hear my song
I'll sing of love to you . . .
and love, as it grows
can fill the empty skies
like forgiving eyes
Let our voices rise together

You are the song
That the world should be singing
Voices could rise and fill the air
You are the happiness
We all might end up bringing
If we could only learn to share

All in all we've had a taste
Of the good and the bad
Times spent in love
Were the best that we've had

If I can make you cry
If I can fill your eyes with pleasure
Just by holding you
In the early hours of morning
When the day that lies ahead has
Not quite begun . . .

If I can make you smile
If I can move you close
To laughter with a word or two
When your day has been filled with strangers
And the castles that you build
All tumble down

Oh well, that's enough for me
That's all the hero I need to be
I smile to think of you and me
You and I
And how our pleasure makes you cry

When my world becomes
     too much for me
And I've had my fill of its schemes
I reach back into its history
And recall my childhood dreams

With my love for how things used to be
And a once imagined friend
I will find a time that's right for me
Try to find a better end

henever I need
To leave it all behind
Or feel the need to get away
I find a quiet place
Far from the human race
Out in the country . . .
Whenever I feel
Them closing in on me
Or need a bit of room to move
When life becomes too fast
I find relief at last
Out in the country

Before the breathing air is gone
Before the sun is just
A bright spot in the nighttime
Out where the rivers like to run
I stand alone and take back
Something worth remembering

Friends are like music
Sometimes they're sad
Sometimes they're lonely
And need to be told that they're loved
Everyone needs to be loved

Friends are like good wine
And I've had the best
Don't always show it
But no one knows better than I . . .

Friends are like warm clothes
In the night air
Best when they're old
And we miss them most when they're gone
Miss them the most when they're gone

Friends love your good side
And live with your bad
Want you and need you
When no one else knows you're alive

've made myself a way of life
   on tomorrows
holding something new
Try to understand me
  deep inside I'm much like you

I've had my share of broken dreams
  and I've noticed
that you've had yours, too
You should understand me
  deep inside I'm much like you

obody moves me like you do
Your magic just goes on and on . . .

Life is not a love song
But broken hearts will mend
And in the quiet of my room
We might sit and hold the pieces
Love can put things back again
I wish that we could still be friends

ove and I were strangers
'Til you and I were friends
Into the shadows of my life
You brought sympathy
    and sunshine

ove is the warmth
That I've felt
    deep inside you
Sharing the silence
    of the dawn

No one knows me better
right down to the letter
You've got a picture
of my soul
You know all about me
you're the first and the last to
doubt me
Sometimes
I confess and you forgive
You're the reason that I live

My love and I
Learning from each other
Gathering roses
on a rainy do nothing day

My love and I
Listen to each other, touching in silence
While we talk of love with our eyes . . .

My love and I
Turning to each other, live every moment
While the world outside rushes by

Lovers never lose
'Cause they are free
   of thoughts unpure
And of thoughts unkind
Gentleness clears the soul
Love cleans the mind
And makes it free

Happiness is happening . . .
Loveliness is everywhere

I would like to know you
show you around
Keep you warm
    and free from danger
share the secrets I have found
    to be true

Trust in me
I will care for you
Share a grace with you
I'll make a place for you
for you and me

Just an old-fashioned
love song
One I'm sure
they wrote for
you and me

ust an old—fashioned love song
Playing on the radio
And wrapped around the music
    is the sound
Of someone promising
    they'll never go

You'll swear you've heard it before
As it slowly rambles on and on
No need in bringing them back
'Cause they've never really gone

Just an old—fashioned love song
Coming down in three part harmony
Just an old—fashioned love song
One I'm sure they wrote for you and me
To weave our dreams upon
And listen to each evening . . .
To underscore our love affair
With tenderness and feelings
That we've come to know

**I** miss you
Like I never dreamed I could
I never will get over you
Only fooling myself
If I think that I can
Got to find you
Got to bring you back to me
Find you
'Cause I've never known
My world to feel so small
I guess I love you after all

**I** ran away from you
And left you crying
And though I'm back to stay
You think I'm lying
But I've changed my ways
And my wandering days are through
And through it all
I've kept on loving you

With a love for how
   things used to be
and a once imagined friend
I will find a time that's
   right for me . . .

So I run from what
   I've come to be
to a time before my own
'til my friend is standing
   next to me
and I know I'm not alone.

Time was a friend of mine
Back when I was young
And summer was forever
Time, good was your first name
Every day a lesson
With something new to learn . . .

You have shared my life
Like a trusted friend
You have watched me grow old
While this story I have told
Is ending

I never had much money
I never won a race
My jokes don't end up funny
I've had doors slammed
    in my face
But I think you've charmed me
I always hoped that someone would
I never had a love like this before
I never had it so good

**S**ome people
      always complain
         that their life is too short
      so they hurry it along . . .

As for me
I have all the time in the world . . .
   for me, life can be
   a sweet holiday

Sometimes it seems like you and me against the world

When all the others turn their back
And walk away
You can count on me to stay

Remember when the circus came to town
And you were frightened by the clown
Wasn't it nice to be around
Someone that you knew
Someone who was big and strong
And lookin' out for

You and me against the world
Sometimes it feels like
You and me against the world

Life can be a circus
They underpay and overwork us
And though we seldom get our due
When each day is through
I bring my tired body home
And look around for
Me and you against the world

Sometimes it feels like
You and me against the world
And for all the times we've cried
I always felt that God was on our side

And when one of us is gone
And one is left alone to carry on
Well then remembering will have to do
Our memories alone will get us through
Think about the days of me and you
Of you and me against the world

Day after day
I must face a world of strangers
Where I don't belong
I'm not that strong
It's nice to know
That there's someone I can turn to
Who will always care
You're always there

About the Author

Although he's short in stature, Paul Williams is one of the biggest names in the entertainment world today. The status he has achieved as a composer is nearly unparalleled in contemporary music. But Paul's songwriting abilities highlight only a portion of his creative talents.

Lyricist, actor, comedian, T.V. personality, scriptwriter and concert performer, Paul Williams has always had entertainment in his blood. He graduated from class clown in Long Beach, California to the skies over Albuquerque, New Mexico, where he performed as a stunt parachutist. Nearby theater productions provided an outlet for Paul's creativity, and he spent seven years acting in plays, films and television programs between New Mexico and Hollywood.

While shooting a movie on location for an extended period of time, Paul picked up a friend's guitar and began "inventing" chords to relieve the boredom between scenes. Since he was far too inexperienced to play other people's songs, he had only one alternative to continue playing: to begin writing his own songs.

The rest of the story is music history. One of the world's most magical songwriters was discovered — first by a handful of people and later by a worldwide audience. Paul's recognition as a giant in the industry is well-deserved. He has been the recipient of numerous awards, including an "Oscar" for best song ("Evergreen") and Academy Award nominations for "Nice to Be Around" and the film score for "Phantom of the Paradise." Four of his compositions have been awarded gold records, including "We've Only Just Begun," "Old-Fashioned Love Song," "Cried Like a Baby" and "Rainy Days and Mondays." And he has had the pleasure of hearing his music performed and recorded by a variety of musical stars, including Barbra Streisand, Helen Reddy, the Carpenters, Three Dog Night and Seals and Crofts.

Paul Williams' talent and personality have helped him play a beautiful part in the lives of millions of people: a special role that is sure to continue for many years to come. And as Paul says himself, "You can't have too much beauty in your life."

ACKNOWLEDGMENTS